Guess What Rocks Do

Barbara Rinkoff

illustrated by Leslie Morrill

Lothrop, Lee & Shepard Co.

New York

By Barbara Rinkoff

GUESS WHAT GRASSES DO
Illustrated by Beatrice Darwin

GUESS WHAT TREES DO
Illustrated by Beatrice Darwin

GUESS WHAT ROCKS DO
Illustrated by Leslie Morrill

Printed in the United States of America.

1 2 3 4 5 79 78 77 76 75

Library of Congress Cataloging in Publication Data

Rinkoff, Barbara.
Guess what rocks do.

SUMMARY: An introduction to the characteristics, uses, and scientific and practical value of rocks and minerals with a discussion of beliefs and customs concerning them and suggestions for collecting.
[1. Rocks. 2. Mineralogy] 1. Rocks—Juvenile literature. 2. Mineralogy—Juvenile literature. I. Morrill, Leslie, illus. II. Title.
QE432.2.R56 552 74-16111
ISBN 0-688-41678-0
ISBN 0-688-51678-5 (lib. bdg.)

To Carol and Richard Rinkoff

Have you ever tried to skip a flat rock
across water,
used a heavy rock to anchor your boat,
or climbed high rocks in the park?
Rocks are so familiar,
you may never have given them a thought.
They have been around for millions of years—
much, much longer than people.

Early men and women used rock caves
for shelter from the sun and rain.
They used rocks as weapons,
to get food and to fight off their enemies.
They learned to strike stones together
to make sparks to start a fire
for cooking and for warmth.

The Bible says that rocks were used
to measure weight. The scale would balance
when the grain or oil or whatever you were buying
weighed the same as the stone.
Flat stones were used to write on,
since there was no paper. And, in times of war,
stones were scattered over the enemy's fields
so that farmers could not till their land
to grow crops, and the enemy
would not have food.

The ancient Egyptians believed that the tomb
was the everlasting home of the dead,
and that it should be built of the strongest material
to shelter them for eternity.
So the Egyptians built pyramids of stone
as tombs for their dead rulers.

The ancient Greeks used stones called "calculi"
to add with and subtract.
They called this "calculating"—
a word we still use in mathematics today.

In ancient Rome,
before clocks and watches were invented,
time was told by a sun dial.
The sun dial had a face of flat stone
because stone was strong enough to withstand
all kinds of weather. The sun's shadow
moved around the numbers on the stone
and measured the time of day.

The earliest people in North America, the Indians,
used stones in other ways.
By tying rocks to sticks,
the Algonquins made hammers and axes
and used them in making dugout canoes.
They burned out the inside of tree trunks
and then chipped away the charred wood
with the stone ax and stone hammer.

Hopi Indian women
sat together in groups of three,
each with a stone of different roughness in her hands,
grinding corn on a flat stone worktable.
The first woman ground the corn to a coarse meal.
The second woman, using a smoother stone,
ground the meal still finer.
The third woman used the smoothest stone
to finish the grinding process.

Indians placed stones in patterns
to mark their trails.
They put stones inside a gourd
to create a rattle
for making musical sounds
in their singing and dancing ceremonies.

In colonial days in America,
each schoolchild had a thin piece of stone called slate
to write the lessons on.
Today we use paper, but in our classrooms
we still use slate for a blackboard.

Each colonial village had a miller
who ground the farmers' grain,
taking part of the flour as payment for his labor.
He sold the flour to bakers
who made it into breads and cakes to sell.
The miller's most prized possession
was his millstone.
Without a good stone, he would have been unable
to grind the grain into flour.

The early settlers used stones
in front of doors to serve as steps.
They cleared the ground of rocks
so that the land could be tilled and planted.
Then they built stone walls along their property lines
to show where their property ended.

Stones and rocks are necessary
to other creatures besides people.
Have you ever watched a seagull eat a clam?
It flies close to the water,
picks up a clam,
soars high into the air,
then drops the clam on the rocks
where it breaks open so the gull can get at the clam.
And some birds swallow small stones
that remain in their gizzards
to aid in grinding up the hard seeds that they eat.

If you pick up a stone from the ground
you might find that it has been the roof
of some insect's home.
And if you look into the spaces
in a stone wall
you may find the homes
of snakes, chipmunks,
or rabbits.
Stone caves sometimes house
wolves, bears, and bats.

As you can see, people and animals
have all used rocks
in many ways.
But besides being useful,
rocks were sometimes thought to be magical.

In India, a stone with tree-like markings
represented the God Vishnu.
It was the custom for Brahmin men
to own one of these stones and pray to it daily
to please the God.
A household without this special stone
was looked down upon.
The food prepared in such a house
was considered not fit to eat.

The Brahmin bride placed
her right foot on a stone
and said that she would be firm as a rock
in her love for her husband.

Ancient Danes stood on stones
when voting for leaders
to show that their loyalty would be
everlasting, like a rock.

Ancient Mexicans carved stone gods
and placed them around their fields
because they believed this would encourage
their crops to grow.

In Africa, along the upper Nile, often the chief
was a rainmaker. He kept a pot of "rain stones"—
amethyst, rock crystal, and aventurine.
To make rain, or to stop it,
he would put the stones in water
and wave a special cane at the clouds
while he chanted to tell the clouds
which way he wished them to go.

In Papua, people would drive a stone
into the bark of a tree when a baby was born
to unite the baby's life
with the tree's life.
If the tree grew tall and strong,
they believed the baby would too.
If the tree withered and died,
so would the child, they thought.

The long, shaped stones on the Banks Islands,
north of Canada, were called
"eating ghosts." People believed
that dangerous and powerful ghosts lived in them.
If your shadow fell on such a stone,
the ghosts could draw out your soul
and you would die. When the owner of a house
went away, he set that kind of stone in the house
to guard it from enemies and thieves,
since no one would dare
to let his shadow fall upon the stone.

Old Scottish witches were said
to be able to create wind by dipping a rag in water,
then hitting it three times on a special stone.

The kings of Scotland were always crowned
upon the Stone of Scone. This stone was carried off
by the English king in the year 1296,
and placed in Westminster Abbey in London
where it still lies today
beneath the royal coronation chair.
When a new ruler is crowned,
the stone is there to show that he or she
will rule over Scotland as well as England.

In Ireland there is a very famous stone.
People come from all over the world
to kiss the Blarney Stone
because it is supposed to give those who kiss it
the talent of being able to "sweet-talk" anyone!

Each month of the year has a special stone.
Wearing your birthstone in rings, necklaces,
and bracelets is supposed to bring you good fortune.

You may not believe that rocks are magic,
but they are very important to you.
For instance, it is mostly crumbled rock
that makes up the soil where
beef and dairy cattle graze
and farmers grow their crops.

And every day, rocks are mined
and their minerals removed.
From these come metals—like copper,
which is made into things like electrical wiring,
and gold and silver, which have many uses,
such as money.

You use minerals every day without thinking.
The yellow paint on your wall gets its color
from chromium; the chrome on your refrigerator
comes from the same mineral.
Your pots and pans may be aluminum,
which comes from a mineral.
Your family's car, machines, and tools
are made of iron and steel,
which come from minerals.

Other minerals have no metal,
or are not used for the metals in them.
One such mineral is garnet,
which we put into jewelry.
Another is graphite, which you know as
the "lead" in a lead pencil.
Still another is the salt you sprinkle on your food.

The sand on our beaches is mostly crumbled
quartz, the most common mineral on earth.
Quartz sand makes sandpaper
and is also used in making glass.
Quartz crystals are melted to make lenses.

Natural gas, oil, and coal
are special kinds of minerals.
They provide us with heat and power.

Rocks do something else too.
They give us clues
to the history of life on our planet.
Layers of rock show how our earth was formed.
And in some rocks you can find fossils—
impressions of the remains
of animals and plants that lived long ago.
From such layers of rock, and from the fossils,
scientists can tell what life was like here
millions of years ago.

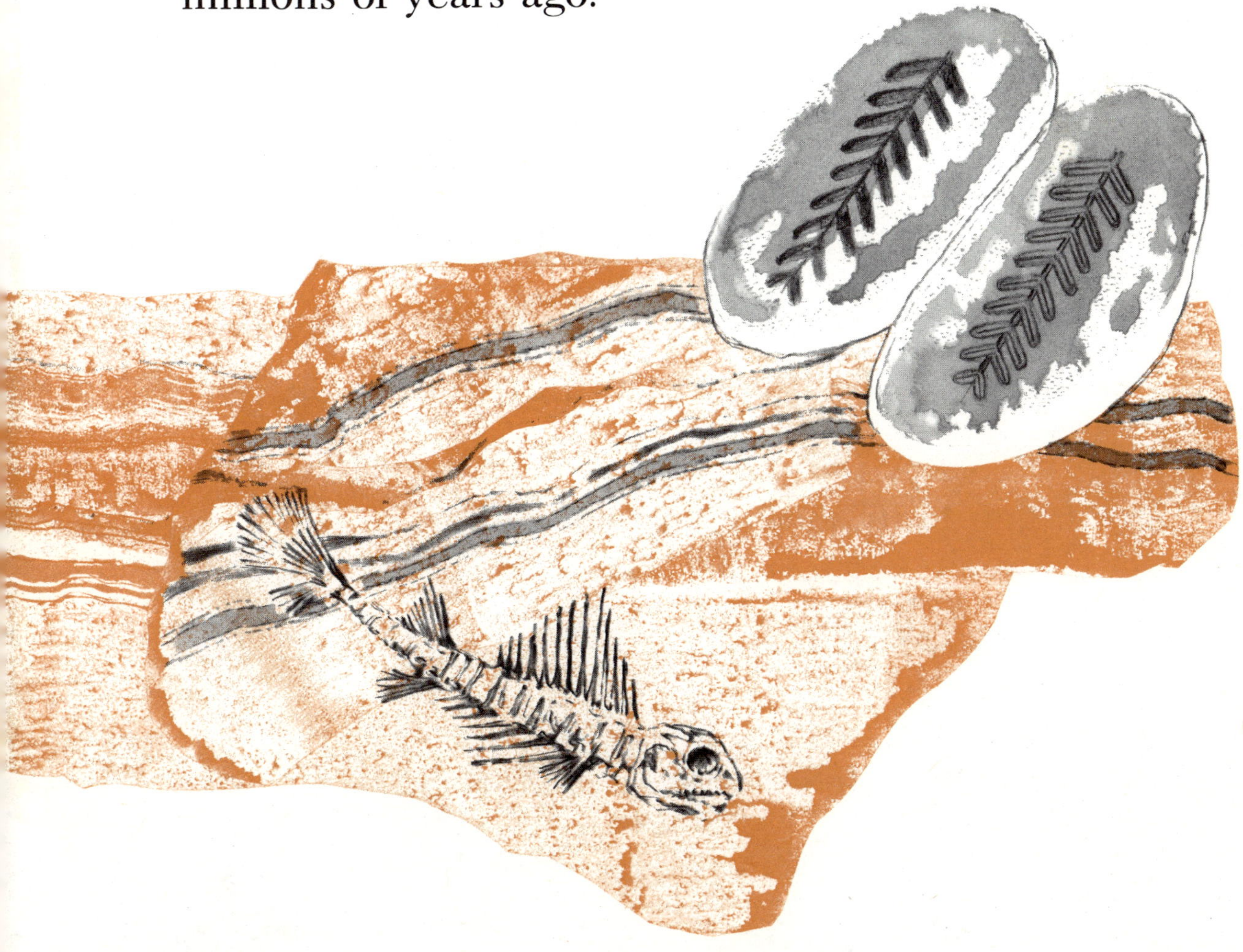

On television you may have watched the astronauts
collecting rocks on the moon.
They brought the rocks back to Earth
for scientists to study
to learn how the moon was formed.
Perhaps the moon rocks will unlock the secrets
of the creation of our solar system.

Even if you can't be an astronaut,
able to find moon rocks to study,
you can start a rock and mineral collection
here on Earth, and
learn how valuable they are to man.
There are over a hundred kinds of rocks
and about fifteen hundred types of minerals.
You can find them yourself in lots of places, like
riverbanks, stream beds, where new roads
are being built, and at the ocean.

Or you can buy them,
or swap them.
You can get books and magazines
telling you where to look for specimens,
and your state will send you
a guide to its mineral deposits.

If you have a book
with pictures of rocks and minerals,
you can identify what you find.
If you want to break up rocks,
you'll need a hammer and a special chisel.
Don't forget to wear goggles
to protect your eyes from flying chips.
Heavy gloves will protect your hands
from cuts and bruises,
and a large bag is helpful
for carrying specimens home.

You can learn to identify and label specimens,
and perhaps even to cut and polish them.
Or maybe you'll want to collect
minerals that glow
in colors like brilliant orange,
blue, and green
when you use a special light on them.
You may want to start your own club
of rock hounds!